MW01135328

Mane Batalla
August 2018

The "What" About Faith

A Guide to Knowing God Every Day

by John Quinata,
Founder of Our Father's Grace Ministries
San Diego, California

Crystal Pointe Media, Inc.
San Diego, California

The "What" About Faith

By John Quinata

Copyright © 2015

Published by Crystal Pointe Media, Inc.
San Diego, California

ISBN-13: 978-1516861958
ISBN-10: 1516861957

Cover Design by Victoria Vinton

Table of Contents

Dedication

*Dedicated to my loving wife Irene, my son John Vincent,
and my daughter Cara Lynn.*

Having you in my life is a clear testament of God's love for me.

Acknowledgements

Thank you to my daughter, Cara Quinata for your original cover design, format for this book, creating the "About the Author" page, and for your technical and heart felt support. You are an inspiration for our family ministry and I love the depth of your faith in serving God.

Thank you to my son, John V. Quinata for being the pillar of strength and encouragement for our entire family. You are a guiding light in your dedication to the service of others.

Thank you to my wife, Irene Quinata for your technical assistance on this book, and, as always, for your unconditional love, support and your belief in me.

Thank you to my dearest friend, Christine Davis, who is the Director of Catechetical Ministry, San Diego, California. You are my church family, and a true spiritual light. Thank you for your support of this book.

Thank you to Sister LaVern Olberding, Franciscan Peace Connection, La Mesa, California. You are a powerful mentor, and a heavenly example of service for me.

Thank you to Pastor Bob Eusebio II, Living Stone Ministries, Daly City, California. You are a blessing to our family and my ministry.

Thank you to Tina Erwin and your entire staff, Crystal Point Media, Inc. I appreciate your help in walking me step by step through the process of the publication of this book. Your professional knowledge and personal touches were invaluable.

Thank you all for being such blessings in my life, in Jesus' name!

Clearly more of my Father's Grace!

Testimonials

"John Quinata is one of the most spiritual people I know. He will not only show you how to find God in every aspect of your life, he will also enable you to see the hand of God in all of nature. This book is truly a testimony to his glorious adventure in faith as guided by the Holy Spirit."

Christine Davis,
Director of Catechetical Ministry,
San Diego, California.

"Minister John Quinata's *The "What" About Faith* helps in developing our discipleship and faith to follow Christ by showing ultimately how God's plan enters our lives, giving us the opportunity to know Jesus Christ as our Lord and Savior. A must-read for non- and new believers."

Bob Eusebio II,
Pastor of Living Stone Ministries,
Daly City, California

Foreword

Hindu mystic Sri Ramakrishna frequently shared stories with his devotees to ignite their understanding of and zeal for achieving his followers' greatest potential.

The story of the woodcutter and the sage is one of my favorites: There once lived a poor woodcutter who couldn't earn a decent living because the trees available to him were not of very good quality. A sage lived in the same forest as the poor woodcutter, and one day the woodcutter approached the sage, almost in desperation. The sage looked at the woodcutter intently. The woodcutter peered deeply into the sage's eyes. His eyes seemed to be saying to the woodcutter, "Go deeper."

The woodcutter decided he would do just that, so he walked deeper into the forest and found a large thicket of valuable sandalwood trees. Now the woodcutter would only need to work once a week.

In time, the woodcutter reflected on his interaction with the sage. The words, "Go deeper" would not leave him. Once again, he decided to venture even deeper into the forest. This time, the woodcutter discovered a silver mine. *How amazing*, he thought to himself. *Now my worries are truly over.*

More time passed, and again the eyes of the sage came to the woodcutter's mind. Again he heard the sage's message, "Go deeper." The woodcutter decided to search still deeper into the forest. His search paid off: This time, the woodcutter found a diamond mine.

The humble woodcutter was overwhelmed. He realized that all of these gifts had come from the grace of the sage, but only after the woodcutter chose to respond to the invitation to "Go deeper."

Through the years, I've had many enlightening and uplifting

conversations with my friend and colleague "John Q." In almost every conversation, he says something that reminds me of the Hindu mystic and the sage in this story. John has a passion for living every minute of his day to the fullest. He also has a burning desire to kindle similar passion in his family and friends, his Sunday class of budding believers and doers, any strangers and regulars he meets during his daily deliveries, and countless others lucky enough to cross his path.

In this book, with childlike awe, John articulates his adult synthesis of what faith can embody and empower when one chooses to go deeper, and then yet deeper – and still even deeper. He invites us to become conscious of the multitude of external "post-it notes" that correspond to our internal questions about reality, life's purpose, God, truth and so much more.

As you read John's words, allow yourself to go deeper into your own "faith forest" of internal natural resources. Expect to find your own life-giving treasures buried beneath the layers of limiting beliefs, doubt, skepticism, and materialism. Enjoy discovering the spiritual wealth and power your faith has to free you from your impoverished illusions and misconceptions.

LaVern Olberding, OSF
Co-founder and visionary for the Franciscan Peace Connection in La Mesa, CA
www.franciscanpeaceconnection.org.

Introduction

If you are a person who believes in God, this book is for you.

No matter what religion you recognize or which holy days you choose to celebrate, the practice of your faith can be outlined by this very easy guide to recognizing God in your life.

To have religion in your life is to believe in God. From the Latin word "religio-," which means "to believe," all sects of religion have one common denominator: faith. The cultures are different, the languages are different, and even the names or titles are different. But the basis of faith, believing in God, is the same.

To truly live our faith, we must realize God's presence by giving Him our absolute trust and total commitment to our lives as miracles of His creation.

Being alive, enjoying every day and everything around us are God's blessings of His presence. The truth of God's existence is in the recognition of all His creation.

The "What" About Faith

Faith, the very foundation of all spiritual teachings, is often misunderstood. Many definitions all have one common ground: belief. Therefore, faith has a direct connection with all sects of religions throughout the world, from Hinduism, Buddhism, Catholicism, Judaism, and Islam to many other forms of worship.

This book is written with all worldly teachings at heart and demonstrated from the eyes of Christianity.

We're taught that we must first accept faith as not what we know, but instead what we believe. To be a person of faith, you must prepare yourself to believe without asking for proof; the moment you ask to see the facts, your faith has turned into "I'll believe it when I see it." You must have absolute trust and commitment in what you believe without question or doubt – not an easy task for us here in the physical world. But God doesn't ask us to be flawless. Instead, He wants us to see the goal and to work toward achievement through His love, understanding and compassion.

For centuries, it has been man's way that we are God's creation, separate in our beings and striving to learn of Him. To see Him, touch Him and communicate with Him. Taught to have faith that He is out there and can be found, or that upon passing from this life, we'll be received by Him on our arrival into heaven.

Although this is all true, it's also true that we are one and the same. Filled with God's energy of life, love and compassion, I believe that God lives within me as much as I live within His heart. God can be seen, touched and communicated with simply by realizing yourself and who you are in this life.

Many scriptures talk of the "I am" – God's presence. Say the words and realize that is God talking to you, that His presence is within you.

Having faith is believing in life itself. We believe God has created all of life and that His existence is true, so we must look at ourselves and all that surrounds us as the very fact that God is here with us.

To have faith is to react or respond to any situation with hands raised in praise and submission, even as your human desires are different. Part of absolute faith is believing that God is in control and that nothing is put to chance. Sometimes things happen here in the natural world that we react to with instinctive behavior. Other times, we're able to respond logically to external situations.

These are the unrecognized moments of power and strength that God's given us. We overlook these moments and take for granted that *we* dealt with the situation; *we* corrected the problem and moved on, as if we are in absolute control of the moment. Thanks be to God for the wisdom He has blessed us with.

Sometimes there are events in our lives that seem too large for us to bear. Feelings of devastation and uncertainty can happen. It can be confusing and make us feel lost, with seemingly no way to deal with the problem. In these moments, our emotions rise to the surface and add the extra weights of stress and helplessness. At times, a feeling of darkness can consume us, often resulting in depression, sadness and loneliness. But God is still here with us.

The trials, the challenges and hardships of life are moments to regroup and refill your tank of faithful direction in how you're living your life. Keep your faith that all the problems we face come to pass. There has never been a problem that has come to stay.

Pastor Joel Osteen once said, "A pearl is caused by an irritation in the oyster's life, and yet we treasure that pearl as a precious gem once it's been removed and the problem has passed. Be the pearl in your problems of life." Believe that the irritation these moments cause also cause us to grow and emerge as more valuable gems.

Anytime there are questions, concerns and worry, there's also a call to our faith. Remember who we are: children of the Most High God. We are empowered with His strength, wisdom and conviction, created in His image and filled with His breath of life. If your faith is belief in a God of all creation, then a problem here in the mortal world is but a slight adjustment by the Maker Himself. It's God who has placed you on your journey of life. It's God who is in control of your destiny and it is the same God who will support you, guide you, and deliver you from the burden that weighs so heavily on your shoulders. This is our *faith*.

Let God know that you recognize His blessings every day. Let God know that you're thankful for His presence in your life and your love and faith in Him are strong and deeply seated in your soul. It is not enough to say "I believe." Instead, you must see God in everyday life.

When an event in your life goes well, thank God for His favor and grace. Say "thank you" for all the support from the people He has surrounded you with who played a part for your success.

Equally, when you see your neighbor struggling with a daily chore, or you see an elder having trouble crossing the street, don't just wonder internally if they might need help. Know that God has placed you there in that moment so you can help and be a part of their comfort and success. Live God's way each day serving each other as you ask of Him to help and serve you. Look to see God in everything and everyone around you. Your faith is that God takes care of you, that His love for you is that of a father's for his child. Your service to Him is in the part you play to take care of our world and to be there for your peers who need His helping hand. Be God's hands. Be the tool He can call upon to help and serve those all around you who call out to Him. All things on earth are here for you – even we are here for each other. It is a call to your faith, not as words, but as a way to live life.

In scriptures it is written that God is "the light that shines within."

"... in Him was life, and the life was the light of all people, The light shines in the darkness..." John 1:4-5

Sometimes it takes the darkness of night to see the shining light of the stars in the heavens above. In life, it is in the darkest moments that we are able to see most clearly God's light of presence, if only you call to your faith and look for Him. Those very same stars are also shining in the daylight, but they're not seen because of the brightness of the day, and distractions like our jobs, our chores and our obligations. But just as the stars are still there in daylight, the problems and worries are still there throughout the day and the night.

Therefore, you can't only look to God in the darkness of night – of hard times – but every moment of the daylight as well: during our jobs, our chores, our good times and obligations. God doesn't simply take over after your daily grind is done, nor does God spring into action when your smooth days turn into the darkness of night. He is with us always, blessing us in the good times and carrying us in the tough times.

There is no one better than the Creator of all things who knows how to repair breakdowns in your journey of life. Look for His guidance and ask for clarity and direction. Giving thanks and praise for His presence in our lives should be an everyday prayer, for He will never let you journey alone. This is what we believe. This is our faith to live.

There is an old saying that "God helps those who help themselves." This is absolutely true. You can't be idle when it comes to your life.

God wants us to be productive, to achieve and be worthy. To be successful and of value to the world, whether it means you make policy that helps all of society or you're a leader and an inspiration within your own family, preparing the next generations to take over and serve.

All of God's missions are equally important. But you have to understand that they all are *individually* God's missions. Even though it falls on us to work hard to accomplish our missions in life, it's God's direction and design that makes us a piece of the larger puzzle.

Therefore, our faith plays a big part in our striving to do well. While staying in touch with our senses and opportunities around us, we must still raise up our hands to God as we let Him know that we recognize all of this as His will.

Our service to Him becomes our success and happiness. The harder we work to fulfill His direction of us, the more we accomplish and the easier life becomes. This is often referred to as "divine favor." Through our faith, all things are possible. The harder we work with sincerity that it is God's direction and plan, the greater our service becomes for all to benefit from. How we live our daily lives is our faith. It is not enough to say "I believe." We must live the faith each day, recognizing what we believe is God's presence in the world around us.

When things in our life don't go as we planned or when they change unexpectedly, it can be a disappointment or fill us with uncertainty. Take a deep breath – God's spirit of life – and call on your faith. Remind yourself that all you're experiencing is God's plan. Know within your heart that God would never hurt His child without a lesson to learn and an outcome of triumph and success.

As much as unexpected change can seem scary and disappointing, it can also be a stepping stone to new heights of achievement and a better future. If you remember to keep your faith, be positive that God's plan is happening, the changes in your life will be more rewarding for the overall outcome and your future. We must believe that although we live here and now, what we do today has a direct effect on who we become later in life. Remember: God does not let things happen *to* you. He allows things to happen *for* you.

God's direction is never wrong. We only fail when we attempt our journey without Him. It's our journey, but it is by the grace of His guiding hand that we have guaranteed happiness. Faith, every moment of what we believe, every moment of every day we live.

The Grandeur of Creation

How can we see God? How can we live God's way when, until we die, we can't be with Him? If God wants us to have faith in Him, why doesn't He reveal Himself to us? These are three very common questions I hear along the lines of "How can we get closer to God?"

The magnificence of God is everywhere. It only takes a moment of your time in any given day to recognize His presence in your life. From the simplest forms of creation to the most complex harmonies of life, God can be recognized if you pause long enough to take a breath and absorb the vastness of His creation around you.

Beginning with yourself, realize that you are God's greatest creation. Your abilities to see, hear, taste, smell and feel are an everyday miracle that we take for granted. The function of our bodies is in perfect harmony, allowing us to walk, talk, breathe and think without consciously having to direct any commands to do those tasks.

Your mind has the ability to absorb and retain an infinite amount of factual information while also being able to create, through imagination, an unlimited number of abstract designs. A wise man once said that imagination is God's garden of creation. Look around you and see the grandeur of God's garden.

Consider your heart. Without it there is no life. Continuously pumping vital nutrients and oxygen throughout every cell of your body, its ability to keep up with your activities all day, every moment, without a switch to turn it on or having to plug it in is in itself a clear sign of God's presence within you. The energy your heart uses to beat is the source of life for all creation. In reference to God's presence within us, we call this the Holy Spirit: life's energy itself.

In studying religions across the globe, the idea of the Holy Trinity is common. "Holy," meaning "sacred," and "trinity," meaning "three united." In Christian doctrine, the Holy Trinity is the Father, the Son, and the Holy Spirit. The Father is God, the Creator of all things. The Son is the manifestation of God in physical form we know as Jesus. The Holy Spirit, defined as "sacred breath," is literally "life's energy itself." All of creation contains energy of some form and the visible movement of this energy is simply the Holy Spirit – life in constant motion.

How can we get closer to God? Recognize that there are five physical signs of the Holy Spirit. All five signs affect you every day without exception, and they are proof of God's presence here in the physical world.

The five signs are:
1. Wind
2. Fire
3. Water
4. Rainbow
5. Smile

Let's look at these signs one at a time so we can clearly understand what they mean to us in our everyday lives.

Wind[1]
Have you ever taken a moment out of your busy day to stand atop a hillside or on the beach to feel the wind blowing against your face? Have you ever noticed the trees swaying in rhythm, almost dancing together as the wind blows by them?

---

[1] John 3:8, Acts 2:1-2

The wind carries flower pollen and seeds to new locations to start new lives. Birds and butterflies need the wind to help lift them into flight. Have you ever gone on vacation and needed an airplane to get you to your destination? As you look to the skies watching your child's kite catching the wind to stay in the air, have you ever wondered where the wind is coming from and where it's going? Think about the use of a fan to help cool you down on a hot summer day, or the homerun that leaves the field carried by the wind. Your sails fill with wind, allowing you to steer your boat effortlessly as you journey across the waters. The toy pinwheel spinning out of control creates a show of absolute delight on a child's face. How about your own breath? All living things must breathe to stay alive.

This is the wind. The Holy Spirit, life's energy itself, the sacred breath of life.

Fire[2]

How important is fire in our everyday lives? From the sun to heat our world to the bonfire to give us warmth on a cold wintery night. During a storm the fantastic show of lightening streaking across the night sky, illuminating all of earth below to our enjoyment of the powerful light show. For cooking our foods, whether it is a routine breakfast or a party at the barbeque, warm food is so much more enjoyable than raw eggs or cold uncooked chicken. At the flick of a switch, we have light, fire contained within a glass bulb.

What about our own inner fires of emotions: love, passion, the drive of determination in sports competition? The microscopic molecules of creation, all moving at different speeds of vibration, creating different levels of heat – this is what determines whether rock is solid mass or a liquid flow of molten lava. Even the simple heating of water for a hot cup of tea demonstrates how important fire is to us every day.

Water[3]

---

[2] Exodus 3:2, Acts 2:3-4
[3] Revelation 22:1, John 7:38

15

According to New World Encyclopedia, as much as 78% of the human body is water. Beyond three days without drinking water, the human body begins to die from dehydration.

The earth is made of approximately ¾ water to ¼ lands mass. The constant cycle of evaporation and rainfall feeds the mountains and the plains creating life- sustaining vegetation. The rivers become full so they can run downstream, carrying food sources allowing animals of all species to take their turn feeding and drinking from the life-supporting water as it flows continuously to our oceans, which also supports endless varieties of God's creatures.

All of creation has some degree of moisture contained within its own design, and all of creation relies on the rejuvenation of that moisture to continue to exist. From the teardrops in your eyes to the refreshing plunge into a swimming pool, water is an everyday necessity of life.

Rainbow[4]

We all know exactly what a rainbow is. The combining of sun rays with the falling rain, God paints an incredible show of color shaped in an arch, high above our heads as we gaze into the sky with excitement and awe.

But the show of color doesn't stop there. After the rains, there are beautiful blue skies and white puffy clouds left behind. The dark to light shades of green in all the landscape around us. The May flowers that the April showers have produced as a multicolored backdrop for all of us to walk through.

How about the clothing we wear? From bold to pastel colors made from dyes to inks to natural fibers and the colors they make up. Look around at the people that surround you, blonde: blue eyes to redheads and green eyes, even the colors and individual shades of our skin tones. Walk into a classroom at your child's school. The walls all around you are a work of art. Their teachers work so hard to create a fun colorful atmosphere for their students.

---

[4] Genesis 9:13, Revelation 10:1

16

The rainbow of God's creation of color is literally everywhere you look and any place that you don't look. From black and white striped zebras to peacocks with tail feathers spread with pride. Our own creativity as art to God's vastness of creation in places like Yosemite National Park, is full of color. See the sunrise to sunset, the different shades of black and white under the glow of the full moon. Color is one of the clear signs that the Holy Spirit is here with us.

Smile[5]

Most often a spontaneous, unconscious show of joy, excitement, an unexpected delight is the smile. At times, it can accelerate into laughter which can infect others all around you. Soon, absolute joy and uncontrollable laughing fills the room with friends and family hysterically enjoying the moment.

Have you ever experienced an infant or baby displaying delight, even when you know that the child is too young to understand what was just said or what just happened? That smile on the child's face gets an immediate response by all the adults around the child, and the adults begin to smile and enjoy the moment as well.

This is a God-given energy from within us, of pleasure and joy that displays itself outwardly on our faces. To greet a stranger with a smile and a "good morning" or "pleased to meet you" creates a mirror effect as the stranger spontaneously returns the favor of good feeling to you. Together you share in the moment of pleasure.

Joy, happiness, and delight are all an extension of the smile, a physical display of God's living energy within each and every one of us. We are an example of creation, God's presence here and now.

These five signs of the Holy Spirit's presence in the physical world are daily proof of God in our lives. The examples given here are only a handful displaying how we can recognize His presence among us, but they clearly show just how easy it is to see, feel, and know God's energy of life all around us.

---

[5] Psalms 126:2, Job 8:21

If you pay attention, the examples are endless. These five signs do affect us every single day of our lives and God does this on purpose to show us how easy it is to have faith in the fact that He is here.

Give yourself a breath of His blessings each day and recognize all five signs, at the moment that they happen, and you'll be surprised at how often during your day His light of presence shines on you. Suddenly, you will realize that it is not moments of your day, but constant, all day, every moment of your life.

This is how we can get closer to God. This is the answer to recognizing God's presence in our lives.

In the Nicene Creed we pray, "I believe in the Holy Spirit, the Lord and giver of life..." Defined as "sacred breath," the Holy Spirit is life's energy itself. The actual *sacred breath of life*.

Remember that God has promised to never let us journey alone. See your life and the world around you as His presence with us, for this is our Father's grace.

The Balance of Life

Balance: Equal representation of opposites.

Here in the physical world, there are always two sides to everything. This is what can be called the *rule of natural creation* or the *laws of balance*. For every start there is a finish. Every beginning there is an end. If there is truth, there is false.

Although God has created everything in our world, you must understand that the moment He made hot there became a cold. The moment He created up, down was made. The same idea applies to yes and no, black and white, night and day, and so on. For every cause there is an effect. This is how the balance of natural creation came to be.

Often I've heard questions such as "Why does God allow bad things to happen? Why does He create war? If God created everything, then He must have also created the devil, right?"

God is a God of all good. The God we know in our hearts and worship with our faith is a God of all good, incapable of creating bad. It is by this law of natural balance that the bad or evil things have come to be. God creates good, but if we fail to follow Him, we create bad. The simple fact that you can be right immediately creates the idea that you can be wrong. Bad things that happen or evil things

19

in our world are often related to the devil. Did God create the devil? No, but because of the natural law of balance, if there is good in our world, there also is bad.

In an attempt to explain the devil, let me give you this to think about. In the first chapter of this book you read that God lives within each and every one of us. We live here in the physical world with God's energy of life we call the Holy Spirit. The devil would then be the evil misconception of the life energy within those of us who don't understand or recognize God's presence. If you relate God to "the Light that shines within," then the devil would be seen as "darkness within." You can measure light because of its different degrees of intensity. Dark, however, cannot be measured; dark is just dark. If it is not so dark, it is only because there is some degree of light present. Dark is simply the absence of light, as the devil is simply the absence of God. Therefore, God does not create the evil in our world. These are simply things taking place without the realization of God's presence.

> I have come as light into the world, so that everyone who believes in me should not remain in darkness. *John 12:46*

The existence of evil is a fact here in our world, but if we strive to live with faith in God then we limit and can eliminate the evil events we associate with the devil. In the Lord's Prayer, it is written "Thy kingdom come, Thy will be done on earth as it is in heaven." Heaven is the spiritual home of God while earth is the physical home of the very same God. The opposite of heaven doesn't have to be hell. The next time someone says to you "let me play the devil's advocate," tell them "No, there is no room in my life to recognize the devil's presence." Remember, the devil can only exist in places that there is no God.

> Submit yourself to God, resist the devil and he will flee from you. *James 4:7*

The God we love and worship is an all-understanding and forgiving God. We as humans have been blessed with the ability to make intelligent decisions. What separates us from all other forms of life here in the physical world is our ability to choose. All other forms of life respond instinctively in their behavior.

Unfortunately, as humans with this ability we often make bad choices or mistakes in the execution of our decisions. Fortunately, our faith is in a God of absolute forgiveness. What is important to God about our decisions is not whether we got the answer right or wrong. What God cares about is how we use the outcome of our answer despite it being right or wrong.

For example, if your answer to any given question is right, did you use the advantage for your own personal gain or did you use it to help lift others so they too have an advantage in life? If you got the answer to the question wrong, did you give up to depression and failure or did you correct the answer and share what you learned with others so they could avoid your mistake? Your sincerity with how you used the outcome of the decision is what matters to God.

The laws of balance also apply to each and every one of us. Whatever our strengths are, someone else experiences those same qualities as weakness. What we have as our weakness, someone else uses as their strength. It is part of God's plan that we help each other in this journey of life, that we love each other as we love ourselves. After all, if my faith is that God lives within me, then God also lives within you. Helping each other not only makes our journeys smoother, but it also serves God directly in that the love He gives to us He wants us to share with all His creation. This is what keeps our existence in balance and in harmony with the rest of God's world. Remember that in accordance with the laws of balance, the more you give, the more you shall receive.

You can apply this rule of balance to everything in our existence. For every ocean there is a desert. For sweet there is sour. The canopy of a tree is mirrored by its roots. The opposite of physical is spiritual.

Because this is the rule of life, there must also be an exception to the rule. If faith is "believing without asking for proof," then there must be proof to help you believe. That would be God's grandeur of creation. If we believe in a spiritual world full of love and everlasting happiness with God, then most certainly we live in a physical world that He made, full of the very same love and happiness with God.

Choose to recognize God all around you. As hard as you work through your faith to live with God, look to see God living here with you.

It's interesting that most of us view death as the end of life. Life as we know it here in the natural world has many limits, one of them being time. We are taught from a very young age that when you die you go on to live in heaven. Absolute happiness, good health and everlasting time are the promise of God Himself. If this is what you believe, then wouldn't you agree that death would be the beginning of life with no limitations? You would never have to face illness again. Eternal peace and happiness would be your life throughout everlasting time. Once again, as humans, our emotions rise to the surface. Although this response is understandable, we mourn the loss of our loved ones instead of celebrating their new eternal lives.

There are spiritual teachers who interpret this from a very different point of view. The example they use is that when you are asleep, you no longer are aware of this world. You enter a deep state of dreaming, and for the moment, you actually are there in your dream wherever it takes you. It is the bottom of the ninth inning, the bases are loaded, the crowd is cheering at the tops of their lungs, the score is tied and you are the batter. You are there as big and real as life itself. Physically and emotionally you can feel the air around you, the energy of the moment, when suddenly you wake up and realize it was just a dream.

This is the lesson these teachers use to explain the transition of our physical death to everlasting life. Instead of actually dying in this life, we wake up to realize it was all a dream and now we find ourselves in heaven living life with all our faith and hopes a reality. True life is given to us through our death, fulfilling our yearning for God and everlasting love.

So dream big and with confidence that God is holding you in the palms of His hands. It can give such comfort that you can dream this life to the fullest, knowing that when you die, you will wake up in His presence and in a world of love, peace and timeless life. This is what faith is all about.

Creation versus evolution is an argument that has lasted ages. Our faith tells us to trust in God and all His magnificent creation from our own world to the universe above. Creation from an imagination with no limits and yet so exact in individual detail that it allows the very existence of all to survive.

His abstract designs of life itself, from the bizarre creatures below the surface of the oceans to the animals, which survive the vast African tundra, are fascinating. We wonder about the birds that soar overhead, or the ostrich and penguins, which don't fly at all. We are intrigued with the whale and porpoise, which are sea life but are not fish. His plants thrive on lush tropical rainforest or the cactus that bears the brutal conditions of dry desert hot lands. Every surviving life form, no matter where or what the conditions they face, seems to be able to conform so its own physical design can thrive on what God has provided for it to exist. Perfect creations, so diverse in their makeup and yet all are driven by the same single source of life's energy we call the Holy Spirit.

In addition to all the evidence of God's hand in creation, there's also evidence of evolution. The discovery of fossils raises many questions about how life could continue without the ability to adapt, sometimes to literally change their physical development to survive. There is proof of animals here in our modern world, such as the alligator, elephant, and pelican, which have ancestry dating back as far as prehistoric time. Numerous forms of plant life have been traced back to before man and before life as we know it.

There can be no question that evolution is a fact of life. Through millions of years of change, life has had to adapt and conform to simply continue to exist. However, because of the incredible ability to change along with the absolute will to survive, it's clear that there is a stronger power involved. Life keeps moving forward, using any and all resources to stay alive, even if it means changing its own physical makeup. The limitless design of all life and its will to survive has been called "intelligent design" by those who stand solely on the theory of evolution. *Intelligent design beyond our human capabilities.* Wouldn't you call this God? The balance of life has our God as the cause and the ability to evolve as the effect of perfect creation.

Evidence of evolution can be seen clearly here in the present day. Man and our advancement of technology have produced the telephone, which evolved to cordless and cell phones, from simple television to cable and satellite broadcasting. Man's increase in intelligence has enabled us to invent things such as the combustible engine and computers. All are incredible advancements in technology to enable our communications, automation and outright convenience.

The truth is these so-called advancements are due to man's learning how to use these energy sources, not of our own creation of them. God's energy for all these developments has always existed. We have just evolved in our understanding and abilities to build, for our benefit, what has always been available to us by the grace of God's hand.

So the age-old argument of creation versus evolution can be easily answered by recognizing the fact of perfect balance here in our world. The law of equal representation of opposites demands that evolution could not exist without the intelligent design of God's limitless powers to create.

Prayer

Prayer is simply communication with God. Across the world, no matter the culture, traditions or language, millions upon millions of people practice prayer every day. From very young, most of us are taught to pray by our parents in hopes of beginning faith's formation in our lives. Usually starting with very basic prayers like Grace at mealtime or bedtime prayers, this practice is meant to start a child's thoughts toward realizing God exists and we need to let Him know that we recognize His presence in the world around us.

No matter your age or whether the prayer is memorized, read or freely made up, communication with God is essential to the practice of your faith. Like any talents or abilities you may have, the practice of your work creates focus, confidence and a proficiency in your ability to recognize the everyday demand of you. Living your faith is not different from having to go to work daily, to deal with school studies or the big game in the sport you play. A need to practice every day builds a strength within that allows you, the natural ability to be God's greatest creation.

While God is with us every moment of every day, there is a definite lack of recognition for Him. It seems most often when there is sadness or times of uncertainty people quickly reach out for the God that is missing from their everyday routine to ask for help and comfort.

The more often we acknowledge God's presence, the more naturally we express God's love for life in our everyday person. We become the lessons of the scriptures. We become the grace of God's guiding hand, and often without even realizing it we become the stabilizing factor in many other lives, as is shown by the ministers we follow. In our own way we all are ministers and teachers of each other. Only through the daily practice of our faith can we become better at displaying and living God's way. Prayer is a sure way of acknowledging God's presence here on earth.

Direct communication with God daily not only pleases Him, as it would be for us to be recognized for our achievements every day, but also opens our hearts so that the love of the Holy Spirit, life's energy itself, can pour outwardly to the world around us sharing our love of life with all who come in contact with us. Remember: The more love of life you give to others, the more love of life you gain. This is true from everyone around us who share in our love for life, including God Himself.

It is so very easy to pray to God. The more often you pray, the easier it becomes. Prayer is simply recognizing God, communicating with God, and sharing time with God. Whether it is brief moments in your day or a measure of time set aside specifically for prayer, there is no better way to share your presence here on earth, than with the God whose love for you is so great, He gave you life.

Vocal

There are three ways to pray. Speaking out loud to God is the first way. Reciting written or memorized prayers or just simply talking to God, expressing yourself in the moment are probably the most common ways thought of when the word "prayer" comes to mind. God hears your voice. God is listening for you. What you need to understand is He is with you at that very moment. God is always with us, but a moment in prayer helps us realize His presence as we direct our voice to God, expecting Him to be there.

Would you just randomly start talking to a friend if they weren't there with you? Of course you wouldn't. What you would do is make an effort to pick up the phone or visit them so you can share whatever is on your mind. That is exactly what you are doing when you make time to pray. You consciously are making an effort to be with God and share yourself with Him. It is an actual calling to God just as when you speak out to your friend, they turn, they listen and they respond. God will also turn, listen and respond, answering every prayer every time.

God does answer all prayers. What many of us miss is that sometimes the answer to our prayer is "no." Sometimes the answer to our prayer is no answer at all. A great spiritual teacher once coined the phrase "Some of God's greatest gifts are unanswered prayers." Don't be frustrated by these answers. Stay in faith. God's answers are never wrong. Often His actions allow situations to develop and come full circle so the truth of your answer can now take place. Understand that we are on God's calendar of time. Trust in Him. His work is always what is best for you.

The laws of balance dictate that if there is a direct way to pray, then there is also a misdirected way to pray. We should not ask God to fix everything to allow us to be carefree in the world. A student may pray that God give them an "A" on an upcoming test. You might ask that God relieve the stress of all our problems. Remember that God's grace is a gift to all of us. You never have to earn God's love, His forgiveness, or His guidance. He will provide us with everything we need for all situations we face if we simply open our hearts to Him.

When you live through your faith and recognize God's presence in your life, you allow opportunities for dealing with trials with the absolute trust that God's favor is with you. Pray for His strength and confidence to do your very best on the test you face. Ask for guidance and direction to find resources to resolve problems. Ask to clearly see the direction He wishes you to take, and for the courage and determination to succeed.

Keep your faith. Remember that God is holding you in the palms of His hands. His will is your happiness and success. All you need to do is recognize His presence, acknowledge His blessings and work to live His life within yourself.

This principle is referred to by spiritual teachers as the "realization of God." Achievement of this realization can come in many different ways. The daily practice of communicating with God is the most direct path to strengthening your faith. Without this practice, your strength and resources are limited to human standards, instead of the limitless powers of God.

Speaking from your heart *verbally* is a powerful way to pray. Praying aloud lets you physically hear yourself recognize that God is here with you. It's an expression of faith that pleases God.

Meditation

A second way to pray is to focus your thoughts within yourself. Sit alone in silence, eyes closed, and focus on who you are – yourself, the "I am" within you. Scripture tells us to look within the darkness, the light of God shines within.

In an earlier chapter of this book you read that the power of the Holy Spirit is the life energy that is active throughout your own body. It's energy that causes your heart to pump, allowing blood flow and oxygen to travel throughout your entire being. Energy that also sends the signals from nerve sensors throughout your body to your brain. The sound created from all this activity within your body is similar to when you're standing under the power lines of your own neighborhood. In the quiet of night, you can hear the hum of the electricity in the power lines above you, just as sitting in silence allows you to hear the life-giving energy running throughout your own body.

Some religions teach that meditation is sitting in a quiet setting, reciting a "mantra" or verbal prayer of "om." If spoken in your natural tone of voice and held at that pitch for an extended period of time, you can actually realize the Holy Spirit within you. If you do this, you'll hear the tone of your voice match the sound of the natural energy of life running within your body. Just like you can tune a guitar to a tuning fork or an orchestra to piano, you can tune yourself to the actual sound of God and His life-giving energy within your being.

The realization of God's presence within you can strengthen your faith. As we carry out all the activities of daily life, the life energy of God is constantly moving within us. Look within yourself and promise that each day you'll do a better job recognizing God inside yourself. Dedicate yourself to knowing God personally by realizing that He lives within you.

Meditation is a form of prayer that's practiced to recognize the presence of God within our own spirits. The "breath of life" is actually the energy of the Holy Spirit running throughout our physical bodies.

Contemplation

A third way to pray is through *contemplation*, or *thoughtful observation*.

One time, I took a class of fourth grade students outside to a grass soccer field and had them lie down on their backs in the grass. With their eyes closed, I asked them, "What do you hear?" At first, they described the sound of a big truck driving by, honking its horn. Everyone laughed because the sound had been so loud and obvious, and so entirely on cue.

After the truck drove away, I asked the kids to listen deeply and pay attention to details. "Now what do you hear?" I asked. Suddenly, one girl called out "I hear birds singing!" Another student described the wind rustling the leaves in the trees around us. Others said they could hear children laughing and playing far off in the distance, a dog barking, and even the splashing of water in a fountain that was across the field. Once they took the time to really *listen*, they recognized numerous things happening all around us.

Next, I asked the young kids "What do you feel?" They said they could feel the sun on their faces, the cool, soft grass tickling their necks and ears, and the slight moisture of the ground from its periodic watering earlier in the day.

"What do you see?" I continued. They answered, "The blue sky above us," and described the soft, puffy clouds changing shapes as they drifted by. One child identified the sunlight reflecting off a tree's leaves as they fluttered in the wind, and another excitedly described a pair of hawks soaring high above us.

This is *thoughtful observation*. Throughout your hectic, busy days, take time out like these fourth graders did to recognize the simple, beautiful signs of God's presence around you.

The warmth of the sun on your face and the shimmering of its reflection on the leaves of the trees is *fire*, a sign of the Holy Spirit. The moisture from the ground, the splashing sound from the fountain and the clouds drifting by overhead is *water*, another sign of the Holy Spirit. The cool wind supporting the hawks as they soar high above and the rustling of the leaves in the trees is the energy of the Holy Spirit. The blue sky above with the crisp white puffy clouds and the laughter from children in the distance are all clear signs of the Holy Spirit's presence.

Every day, all five physical signs of the Holy Spirit affect you. When we think otherwise, it's only because we've failed to recognize them, and in doing so, failed to recognize that God is here with us. It's our lack of recognition, not God's lack of presence. Remember: We've been given the gift of choice. Whether we see God and all His glory is our choice.

Hear the crashing waves of the ocean. See the sparkling sun on the surface of the water. Smell the fresh, salty air of the wind as it blows upon your face.

God is present within us. His gift to us is our ability to realize Him and to live with Him in the world He created. Whether or not we recognize His magnificent creation and absolute proof of His presence is our choice.

Contemplation, the third way to pray, means taking time to recognize God's presence. Let God know through your appreciation and acknowledgement that you're grateful for all He gives to us. A simple smile on your face, the thought – or verbally saying – "Thank you, God" pleases Him. It shows that you realize Him and the beauty of His creation.

God's abilities are limitless. We're not only part of His mastery; He created us in His image and filled us with His breath of life. All we need to do is stay connected to the main power source of God's love. We can do this through prayer.

So, What About Faith?

In this book, I've tried to show that faith is not only what we *believe* – it's also what we *know*. Our faith becomes truth when it's demonstrated in how we choose to live every day.

What we believe can clearly be proven as fact if we make time in our everyday lives to live our faith, to see that God created our world to be true. As much as our faith can be questioned, it can also be the answer to any doubt – but only if we live as we believe.

The presence of faith *does not* mean the absence of doubt. However, the more we persevere in living out our faith, the stronger we become and the more clearly we can recognize the visible signs of God's presence.

Faith is what you believe, but if you don't live out that faith, it's revealed as shallow. Just like two plus two always equals four, your knowledge of this has no value if you say two plus two equals five. To say you believe then fail to live that faith means you won't reap the treasures of the life God's given you.

Recognize your life itself as a gift from God. Stop searching for God through blind faith and instead see God in your actual life here in the world. Have faith that there is always a light at the end of every tunnel, but actively seek to see more light than you see tunnel.

God's creation of our world is real – as real as you are here, and as real as you are part of His creation. Look to see God in everything around you. As we recognize the masterful talent of legends like Monet or Van Gough, we can see the personalities of the artists themselves in their paintings. So why is it sometimes so difficult for us to see God in the artistry of the Grand Canyon, or in the incredible diversity of the animals in the world, or in the love and joy we feel from our friends and family around us?

God is the true master of all creations. As artists create visions of beauty on their canvases, God creates living beauty on the canvas of life.

A teacher once told me a story of man whose love for God was so deep that he dedicated his entire life in prayer to God every day. All day long, every single day, he would pray, "Dear Lord, please find me worthy that through my death You will bring me home to live everlasting joy and happiness with You in heaven."

One night while the man slept, God appeared to him in dream. The man, overwhelmed by God's presence, spoke to God and said "Lord, you have answered my prayers and come to take me home with you!"

The Lord asked, "Have you ever traveled and seen how beautiful the rivers and the forest are?"

"No," the man replied. "I spend my days in prayer so You will see my devotion and love for only You."

The Lord then asked, "What about the magnificence of the mountains, or the eagle that soars high above the clouds? Have you ever felt passion after seeing your family's love or joy from hearing a child laugh?"

"No, Lord" the man answered. "I spend my time in prayer, so you might find me worthy to bring home. I pray so that when I die, You will see my devotion and allow me to have everlasting joy and happiness with you in heaven."

The Lord replied, "How can I bring you home to live in everlasting joy and happiness, when you haven't yet learned how to live the joy and happiness of *life*, the gift I've already given you?"

Earlier in this book you read that prayer is direct communication with God, and that it's vital to sharing your faith with Him. However, if you don't live your faith, you're sharing very little for God to recognize. Words are very easy to come by; actions are harder.

Living out what you say you believe takes character and inner strength that often requires sacrifice. Call on that same faith for support and guidance. Ask God to give you the strength and courage it takes to live your faith.

Also, continue trying to do better with *how* you believe. You probably recall your parents telling you "Say what you mean and mean what you say." Take that to heart and *live* what you believe.

It's easy to say "Let's go to the park." But when you get there, take a moment to *see* the park in all its glory. Enjoy the beauty and the fun people have there. Have fun yourself, but be aware of the wind in your face, the bright, saturated colors of the flowers, the laughter of the children and all the good spirits shared by friends.

Take time to communicate with God. Recognize all the beauty that surrounds you. The more you take pleasure in these things as they're happening, the more you can enjoy the moment. This is the part of life that God wants you to know.

Once you can see your life here with God as more than just a faith to believe in, you'll notice that life becomes the truth of what you believe. Even more importantly, your faith will become your life.

Your relationship with God is personal. How you live your life – how you interact with everyone and everything around you – is the measurement of how close you are to God.

Scripture speaks of how vital community is to our service and worship of God. We are the keepers of the world that He made for us. How we treat each other and our world is a demonstration of love, respect and appreciation for life itself, and that is God's presence here among us.

God comes to us in whatever degree of clarity we allow. The more strongly we believe, the louder He speaks. The harder we try to live God's way, the more clearly He shows us the path. Any shortage of God's favor that we experience in life is usually due to our own doubts and questions of our own belief.

Hoping that God is always with you is a very strong element in faith. But trusting that He's always with you is even more powerful, because it rules out the possibility that He's not with you. Absolute faith is the trust that transforms believing without asking for proof into fact, which *proves* your faith to be the truth.

Use the strength of "I am" to guide your life. Remember that He has blessed you with choice. Choose to live His will, and He will allow you to see your life more clearly.

Happiness, success and love have no limitations in God's presence, so why should there be any limit to these in yours? We limit who we are and what we can do. Open your heart to living God's way and your life will become His will, for all to benefit. Your service to others is directly linked to your love of God. The more you love God as you live your life, the more your life will reflect God's love.

Begin your journey with God today. It's never too late to start feeling what's in your heart. Your hopes and dreams are ready and waiting so your life can gain the benefits – the true intention of God's love. The joy and thrill of being alive in a world of unlimited beauty and unbelievable creation is yours, simply by understanding yourself and the realization of God's presence here with you.

God will treat your past, no matter how many times you may have fallen in your faith, with absolute love and total forgiveness. As a father continues to help his child up each time they fall, God will always help us regain our balance so we can continue smoothly down the path He set for us.

Life is a journey, and it's often full of wrong turns. But it also has many different paths to your destination. Stay focused on the drive, and stay strong in your faith. Let God guide you. He created the path He wants you to take, and He also created the roads you might use to regain your sense of direction after wrong turns.

Live your faith and recognize your journey so you can fully participate in God's heaven here on earth.

> "Faith: Being sure of what you hope for and certain of what you do not see." Hebrews 11:1

It's time for you to see. Live and love life. God bless.

> "I asked God to give me many beautiful things so I could enjoy my life. Instead, He gave me my life so I could enjoy many beautiful things."
>
> ~ Author Unknown

Every day all five physical signs of the Holy Spirit affect us. It's our lack of recognition, not God's lack of presence. These signs are God's deliberate way of showing us that He is here and His way of keeping His promise that He will never let us journey alone.

> "As hard as you try to live with God, recognize God living here with you."
>
> ~ John Quinata

Vocal Prayer

Speaking out loud to God helps us realize God's presence as we hear our own voice calling out, expecting Him to be here.

Meditation

Meditation is the realization of God's living energy within ourselves.

Recognize and acknowledge the Holy Spirit's presence within yourself and love life every day.

Contemplation

The third way to pray, *thoughtful observation*, allows us to see, hear, and feel the presence of the Holy Spirit all around us every moment of our day.

The truth of God's existence is in the recognition of all His creation. This is our Father's grace.

Notes

About the Author

John Quinata founded Our Father's Grace Ministries in San Diego to share the love in his heart and the depth of his faith in God.

John has almost 20 years of experience teaching religious education with the San Diego Diocese, focusing on youth ministry. Now, by the grace and blessings he feels from God, John has expanded his uplifting spiritual message to embrace a much larger audience.

John understands that the word of God speaks to each person individually. Therefore, he wrote The *"What" About Faith* as a gateway to learning more about the connection between ourselves and God, and using the power of that connection to help us find our purpose to serve.

John stands apart from the crowd, preaching and living his faith while guiding others to recognize their own faiths as they're building their own personal relationships with God.

Made in the USA
San Bernardino, CA
03 September 2016